Life with Dr. Carolyn Harrell:
A Magnanimous Journey

Dr. Peggy R. Scott

Life With Dr. Carolyn Harrell: A Magnanimous Journey
by Dr. Peggy R. Scott

Copyright ©2010 by Dr. Peggy R. Scott. All rights reserved.

This book or parts thereof may not be reproduced in any form, stored in a retrieval system, or transmitted in any form by any means—electronic, mechanical, photocopy, recording, or otherwise without prior written permission of the author, except as provided by the United States of America copyright law.

Published by Practical Truths Publication
Franklin, Virginia - www.practicaltruths.com

Printed in the United States of America

ISBN 978-0-9830261-0-5

Carolyn

**Carolyn and
Dr. Wanda Davis-Turner**

Marilyn Hickey & Carolyn

Dr. & Mrs. John Cherry

**Rosey Grier, Sr., Carolyn,
and Rosey Grier, Jr.**

Dr. Betty Price & Carolyn

Drs. Betty & Fred Price

Life With Dr. Carolyn Harrell: A Magnanimous Journey

Carolyn with Archbishop Benson Idahosa

Dr. Peggy Scott

Dedication

This book is dedicated to my mother from the heart, the late Mrs. Estelle M. Baker, whose devotion and love continue to give my life meaning and also to everyone who continues to cherish the memory of Carolyn Harrell.

TABLE OF CONTENTS

FOREWORD 1

PREFACE 2

CHAPTER 1

FAMILY DYNAMICS 5

CHAPTER 2

ALCOHOLISM 11

CHAPTER 3

CAROLYN'S DESTINY AND TESTIMONY OF ONE MAN PUT ME DOWN BUT ONE MAN PICKED ME UP 15

CHAPTER 4

TWO SISTERS ON A JOURNEY 21

CHAPTER 5

MINISTRY EXPERIENCE, CHALLENGES, AND LESSONS 29

CHAPTER 6

GOD'S CHEERLEADER TO THE BODY OF CHRIST 39

CHAPTER 7

WHEN IT ALL FALLS APART 47

CHAPTER 8

THE ILLNESS 53

CHAPTER 9

Restoration 63
Epilogue 73
Carolyn, Thanks for the Memories 76
Vignettes—Scenes from the Cutting Room Floor: 97
Biography of Dr. Peggy R. Scott 101

Acknowledgments

I am sincerely grateful to God for the following persons who labored in love to assist me in the sharing of this journey with you:

My contributing editor, Sharifa T. Black, who is the senior fashion writer for *Forever 21* and *Coverings Magazine*.

Paulette Whitfield Black, who is the publisher of Coverings Magazine, for being my publishing director.

My production assistant, Carol Williams, an Adjunct Professor at Chaffey Community College, in City of Ontario, California.

Claudette B. Jones, Vice President of Baker's Home, Inc., for being my administrative assistant.

Foreword

I met Carolyn Harrell in 1984 shortly after I got saved. She took me under her wing and taught me. She was a mentor as well as my sister. She introduced me to women conferences all across the country and she helped our ministry tremendously financially.

She scared me so bad one night while I was visiting her church! She said, "Candi, you are more than a singer, you are a preacher and you're bringing the Word in the morning." I thought my heart would fall out on the floor! I had never preached before. I stayed up all night trying to find a sermon. I finally put something together. I waited nervously—and then she only called me to sing! Boy was I relieved. That was Carolyn. I sure do miss her, but the good news is, I'll see her again someday when we all get to heaven.

~Candi Staton
Recording Artist
Trinity Broadcast Network (TBN) Host
www.candi-staton.com

PREFACE

My sister, the late Dr. Carolyn Harrell, died in December 2002, "out of the blue," or at least it seemed that way to many. This is not a "tell-all" (some things are just for those of us who were there to know) and please do not review this book as a literary work. Instead, read it as if we are two old friends catching up.

God knows my intent in writing this book, the purpose of which is not to point fingers or place blame, and definitely not to brag, but rather to celebrate the life of my sister—Dr. Carolyn Harrell.

Carolyn's life was not without controversy. It was anything but ordinary. A successful female pastor, her life journey included the ups and downs, transitions, failures, surprises, sorrows and joys that are common to many of us. Yes, she had a big life, but she had an even bigger heart.

My only hope is that by sharing "Life with Carolyn Harrell: A Magnanimous Journey" you will see that her life was not in vain. Learn the lessons that her life taught us, and understand how God can use one person's life to create a ripple to touch many.

Dr. Peggy R. Scott

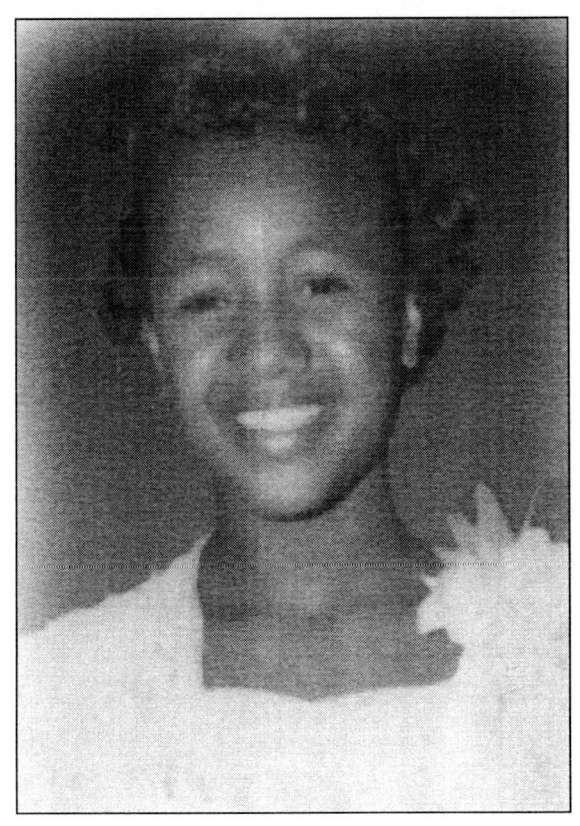

Carolyn Harrell

Age 12

~For we can never for a moment before our God forget your energizing faith, your toiling love, and your enduring hope in our Lord Jesus Christ (1 Thessalonians 1:3 [Williams Bible]).

Chapter 1

Family Dynamics

My life with Carolyn didn't seem to begin unusually. We had two parents, we were raised surrounded by family, and we grew up. It sounds normal enough, until you start to discover the details.

In fact, we were born in the southeastern part of Virginia to two teenage parents who separated after a few years of marriage and the birth of three children. Carolyn, fondly referred to by relatives as "Kitty," was the firstborn. I came along thirteen months later and was followed by our little brother, Matthew, a year later. Each one of us was born prematurely; we came into the world as fighters. From the very start, God was preparing us for the journey ahead.

Carolyn and Matthew, also known as Dicky, were raised in their early years by our paternal grandparents while I was placed with one of our aunts. Even though we were raised apart, our family made sure that Carolyn, Matthew, and I saw each other at least once a week. The three of us were cherished and loved within our new families, but our experiences were very different.

Life with Dr. Carolyn Harrell: A Magnanimous Journey

After the passing of our grandmother, Carolyn was passed from relative to relative within our family. Being handed from house to house that way made it hard for relatives to be aware of the physical and emotional abuse she was experiencing. Carolyn was molested as a child.

Carolyn's story could have easily ended there. She could have taken that situation and used it as a crutch for the rest of her life, but she didn't. Instead, I saw God take a situation that the Enemy intended to destroy Carolyn and turn it into a testimony of deliverance.

I on the other hand, was in a house full of cousins whom I was raised to view as siblings and had a relatively normal childhood. My "mother from the heart" and I had a bond that is difficult to describe. She understood abandonment and being raised by extended family. (She was raised by a maternal aunt after her own mother was violated, as a teenager, in the Mississippi Delta by a Caucasian sharecropper.) Don't get me wrong, I have great admiration and respect for my natural parents, but what my "mom" gave me has as much to do with my makeup as the DNA I inherited from my natural parents. She was there at a time in my life when there was no one else and I thank God for that.

My relationship with my natural parents was understandably rocky. My first memory of my father was when he came to visit me when I was about five years old. I had always wondered why he stayed away so long. It was years later that I found out his absence had been due to incarceration.

I gave him credit for establishing a relationship with us. At the ages of thirteen and twelve, Carolyn and I began to spend our summer vacations in Philly visiting our father. After several summers, we tried to persuade Matthew to come with us. One year he finally gave in, though it wasn't during summer vacation. Matthew and I paid our father a visit, along with one of our cousins. Unfortunately, the experience proved to be too difficult for Matthew and he swore he'd never go to Philadelphia again, and he never did. He died in a train accident a few years later, at the age of fourteen.

The first time I ever saw my natural mother was at our little brother's funeral; even sadder was that someone had to point her out to me. However, Carolyn had grown up knowing her. During trips from Upstate New York, our mother would visit relatives, including Carolyn. But, not me; I never made the list of people to see. As you can imagine, that detail left me feeling extremely rejected.

The years that I spent estranged from my mother, were marked by Carolyn's relentless pursuit to mend mine and my mother's relationship. Eventually, Carolyn's insistence paid off. She talked me into seeing our mother again. I agreed to visit on one condition: if I did not like "those people," I would be free to leave and she would not try to stop me. So, Carolyn and I caught the train and made our way from our father's house in Philly to visit our mother in Peekskill.

As with my father, it was later that the reasons for her actions came to light. It turned out that my mother had not only come to see me when I was younger, but she wanted to take me home with her. According to my mother, she felt that she could not take me back because my extended family had the money, education, and resources she lacked. She feared she could never win against them in court. At the time, she was involved in an abusive relationship and my paternal grandmother was encouraging her to leave us children in Virginia while she got her life together. Even with that information, it still took several years for me to reconcile my thoughts and feelings towards my mother.

Carolyn continued to make an effort to help in the reconciliation of our mother and myself. As you can imagine, some time had passed since my two visits with my mother as a teenager. Carolyn wouldn't be Carolyn without playing "peace maker;" she decided that we should go visit our mother. I was not the least bit excited to make the trip. I protested quite profusely and with good reason. I explained to Carolyn how I had reached out to our mother when I was eighteen. I was in need of financial assistance with my college tuition, and had called to see if she could help. She'd told me that she would do what she could, but nothing ever came of our conversation. When I called again, her husband came to the phone and told me very clearly that my mother had no money to give me and not to call there anymore. Well, you can imagine how devastated I felt. There I was, a young girl who had finally reached out to my mother for help only to be met with rejection, yet again.

Well, Carolyn understood my feelings, but it made no difference to her. She continued to urge me to go to New

York with her and I finally gave in. I was even more surprised that I actually enjoyed our visit. Still, to me it was no different than visiting with someone that my sister wanted me to meet.

The truth is our mother probably did not have the money to give me; she gave birth to thirteen children, after all. And yet, that reasoning never played a factor in how I viewed my mother back then. It would take years for me to understand and identify the weapons that the Enemy was trying to use to destroy us. Rejection was a feeling that Carolyn and I faced often. If not for God's unconditional loving kindness, it may have deterred us from His plan for our lives. Instead, it caused us to fall down sometimes, but we were always able to get back up. God knew the journey we had ahead of us; it was as if He was putting the last piece of the puzzle into place. He had to teach us to have the same loving kindness that he had shown us. Now, I know how to use the Word of God to handle rejection.

Our family history is a shaky one, filled with family secrets and fronts that relatives presented. Some had good intentions, trying to protect my siblings and me. Others' intentions are unclear. We were totally in the dark about what was taking place. There is some truth to the statement that, "What's familiar to you is what seems normal to you." The separation and feelings of rejection, jealousy, and confusion that stemmed from being raised by extended family took its toll on me and Carolyn's relationship. Even in high school, our schools were rivals. We always seemed to be on opposite sides. However, one summer that all changed.

It was a routine day. Carolyn and I were in Philly at our father's house and arguing, as usual. We epitomized sibling rivalry, engaging in yet another fight. I always lost, and still that never seemed to matter. I just could not ever seem to keep my mouth shut. I was selling what we called back then "wolf tickets." What made this particular time different was that Carolyn wasn't buying what I was selling. Instead, she announced, "Peggy I am not going to fight you anymore, I love you." That one declaration changed our relationship forever. I never again viewed Carolyn as an adversary or someone to show anger towards, but rather as someone whom I loved dearly and admired. To this day that feeling has never gone away.

It was Carolyn's love for me that eventually led to my own horrific confession of sexual abuse resulting in teen pregnancy and abortion. For the benefit of the innocent and inquiring minds it was not a violation by an extended family member.

It's funny how you begin to understand "the facts" of your life's beginnings. Looking back, I now realize that mine and Carolyn's lives had to be predestined by God. While our beginning started off rough, like all the trials that followed, we got through it together as sisters, and managed to come out on the other side intact.

Chapter 2

Alcoholism

Carolyn and I both finished high school and decided to attend Norfolk State College. Carolyn was thrown into adulthood sooner than I was. She married her childhood sweetheart early and had to dropout. She had two children, Dion and Tamika. She didn't have the support to raise them and be a college student. During that time, Carolyn was living with her in-laws, which was proving to be more difficult than she'd anticipated. Her husband, an only child, was often the object of the tug of war between Carolyn and his mother.

Carolyn and her family relocated to Baltimore for a time but eventually moved back to Virginia. It was common for southern African Americans to migrate north for new economic opportunities. I myself moved from Virginia to Washington, D.C. and eventually to Philly to pursue a law degree. After the breakup of her marriage, Carolyn moved in with me for a while, allowing her the opportunity to make a decision as to where she and her children were to reside. She found a job with an engineering firm.

As was Carolyn's nature, she gave the guise of everything being okay, however things were anything but. She spent her days as a good employee, but was spending her nights socializing, partying, and drinking a fifth of a bottle of whiskey. Carolyn had turned into a "functioning" alcoholic. To this day I'm still not sure how I missed it. The only explanation I could ever offer was that we traveled in different social circles. I was unaware of how she spent her time after work. It wasn't until she confided in me, years later, that I learned the problem had even existed. Considering the things she endured as a child it is easy to understand her wanting to mask the pain in her life.

Not long after Carolyn moved in with me we were robbed. We returned home one night to find our apartment ransacked. For Carolyn, that was the final straw. I believe it was in that moment that she made up her mind to move to California. Based on her own childhood, Carolyn was adamant that no one would raise her children but her. In an effort to do what was best for them, she packed up Dion and Tamika and headed west.

Unknown to us, the destiny of God was being activated in Carolyn's life. She would never be able to fulfill her life's purpose in Philly.

Even then, Carolyn had big ideas about how she was going to live, what kind of home and environment she would raise her children in. Our family, including myself, used to laugh at her declarations of someday living a life of grandeur. We didn't know it then, but Carolyn was speaking faith into her situation.

She departed for the sunny shores of California. At the time, I wasn't sure if she was being brave or crazy. Carolyn had arrived at the place in her life where God was finally able to use her. She was "broken," and don't you know that's the exact time when God comes in and fixes us?

God had set Carolyn's feet on a path that we would eventually journey together. However, I wasn't ready yet. I wasn't as brave as my big sister, and I still had issues with my mother that I needed to resolve. Now I understand that as God was molding Carolyn into the woman she was supposed to be, he was in turn using her to help mold me.

Life with Dr. Carolyn Harrell: A Magnanimous Journey

Peggy Scott and Tamika (Vaughan) Evans

Chapter 3

Carolyn's Destiny and Testimony of One Man Put Me Down But One Man Picked me Up

Carolyn was on what seemed like the other side of the world, doing "God knows what." In the meantime, I had lost my passion for law and started attending Temple University to pursue a Master's Degree in Social Work. In retrospect it seems a little ironic, but like I said before, God was preparing me to join Carolyn.

You can imagine my amazement when, after a few years in California, Carolyn called to tell me that she had given her life to the Lord. Not one for being at a loss for words, I spewed some foolish and prideful legal mumbo jumbo at Carolyn adding, "That's for you and not for me." She just laughed and said, "I wanted to share it with you."

Carolyn was a devoted and committed servant of the Lord Jesus Christ. It's as if she changed dance partners and began to place herself in His care and dance to His music. She was on fire, enthusiastic, and hungry for the things of God. She began to volunteer at the church; whatever needed to be done she was willing to do. She even went as far as enrolling in business courses, so she could be an asset to the ministry.

It wasn't long before Carolyn's service and devotion to the ministry, showcased through her work ethic, came to the attention of Bishop Robert McMurray. He offered her a position within the ministry and eventually promoted Carolyn to the position of business manager. Around the same time, Charles Harrell, a minister on staff at the church, entered Carolyn's life. Most people don't realize that Charles was Carolyn's second husband.

Carolyn was very much in love with Charles. They married and had one son, Corey. During this time they remained faithful in Bishop McMurray's ministry. When they moved from Los Angeles to Walnut, a suburb east of Los Angeles, Carolyn was introduced to the ministry of Dr. Frederick Price, by her friend Alyce Murray. According to Carolyn, she would slip over to Crenshaw Christian Center as often as she could. The Holy Spirit began to deal with Charles and Carolyn and put on their hearts to begin a ministry in their home. As the ministry began to grow, they began conducting services in the auditorium of the local community college, Mt. San Antonio College. Carolyn was employed at CA-Poly University in the Science Department of the college and took every opportunity to share her testimony of faith with her co-workers. In Carolyn's eagerness to share her love of Christ with others, the ministry they started with evolved into the former Walnut Faith Center, Pomona, California.

Only a few years after Carolyn's salvation, I had my own personal experience with the Lord Jesus Christ, and gave my life to Him. Carolyn and I rejoiced and praised God together. We both were, finally, operating in the will of God. I became consumed with the same fire that Carolyn had! I hungered for the things of God. Carolyn and I became some seekin' sisters. We sought Him day and night.

At Carolyn's urging, I began visiting her in Southern California. I found it to be a beautiful place, not at all like the inner-city of Philadelphia or rural Virginia. I remember how I became captivated with the vision for ministry, the anointing, and the level of teaching. On that trip it became obvious that God had his hand on Carolyn's life.

After my return home, Carolyn called and encouraged me to attend any conference held by Kenneth Copeland, whom I had not heard. At her insistence, I researched and discovered that Indianapolis, Indiana was as close to Philadelphia he was coming. I contacted the travel office handling the hotel and travel arrangements for the ministry partners. I wasn't really a partner, but I was very curious about him. I wanted to know why Carolyn was so anxious for me to hear him.

The trip was an adventure, as was everything that involved Carolyn. I talked a friend of mine into going with me. Neither one of us had ever been to Indianapolis and had only heard Rev. Copeland on the radio. We had started listening to him in preparation for our trip. Well, we arrived in Indianapolis and made our way to the hotel only to find that the travel agency had made an error; we did not have a room reserved at the hotel. Can you imagine our frustration? There we were, miles from home on "some wild goose chase" Carolyn had sent us on and no roof to put over our heads. I was unaware of protocol and did not know that calling Rev. Copeland was not proper etiquette, although if I had, it probably wouldn't have mattered. I needed a place to stay. I made my way to the nearest phone and asked for Rev. Copeland's room. As soon as I was connected, I explained my position to Rev. Copeland and he gave me specific instruction. I was told to look around in the lobby for anyone of his staff in yellow t-shirts with the inscription "Kenneth Copeland Ministries" and ask for Buddy Bell. So, that's exactly what I did; I found the nearest yellow shirt, tapped a man on the shoulder and said, "Excuse me, I am looking for Buddy Bell. I have a message for him from Kenneth Copeland."

The man looked at me strangely and said, "I am Buddy Bell." I proceeded to tell him about my conversation with Rev. Copeland and communicated the instructions given to me. Mr. Bell continued to listen, all the while looking astonished. When I finished speaking, he informed me that "Kenneth Copeland does not talk to anyone before he teaches." I assured him that I had talked to Rev. Copeland and my friend and I got our room. I will always believe that God gave us favor and honored our faith that everything would work out, and it did. I shared that adventure with Carolyn later, since she was the instigator of the trip. Several years later, when Reverends Kenneth and Gloria Copeland ministered at Walnut Faith Center, I was able to share that story with Rev. Gloria Copeland.

Dr. Peggy R. Scott

Peggy Scott

Dion, Corey & Tamika

Dion, Carolyn & Tamika

Laugh at yourself, but don't ever aim your doubt at yourself. Be bold. When you embark for strange places, don't leave any of yourself safely on shore. Have the nerve to go into unexplored territory.

~Alan Alda

Chapter 4

Two Sisters on a Journey

After I completed graduate school and received a Master of Social Work from Temple University, I intended to continue my education. I enrolled in a Doctoral Urban Education program. I was thinking, "What an opportunity," but God had another plan for my life. A few months later I sensed the Holy Spirit leading me to leave the program.

One day, a co-worker gave me a *Guidepost* magazine to read; as I browsed through it, a proverb caught my attention. It read, "God does not want your degrees, diplomas or certificates; he wants your scars to make you whole." I had my confirmation and enrolled in a school of ministry and Bible College.

Carolyn began to visit me more frequently in Philadelphia and was developing relationships with local ministers, such as Dr. Ruth Jackson, Evangelist Barbara Byrd, the late Dr. Charles Waters, Bishop Beatrice Shaw, and others. They urged Carolyn to return to Philadelphia and teach the Word of faith. They could see in Carolyn a true disciple of the Lord and wanted her to join them in the pulling down of strongholds. That's how Covenant Women's Ministry of California began hosting conferences in Philadelphia.

The power of God flowed in those meetings. In one particular meeting, there was a young mother who was distraught over her child's health. The child was in intensive care with a respiratory problem and the doctors had given the family little hope of the child's recovery. The mother had a long vigil by her child's bedside and at the insistence of her mother (Bishop Shaw) she took a break and went to the conference. Bishop Shaw told her that the Spirit of God would meet her there and he did. Carolyn prayed with the young mother and gave her specific instructions, to go back to the hospital and what to whisper in the baby's ear. We praised God as the report came back that the baby had come out of intensive care and was doing fine. I remember in another meeting the Holy Spirit revealed to Carolyn to financially support a young ministry for six months, paying their monthly lease and expenses as they worked in the inner-city to break up the fallow ground.

The Covenant Women's Ministry (CWM) team included Rev. Denotra Johnson, Rev. Sandra O'Neal, and other California ministers. Rev. Jean Perez of Ablaze Ministries, Rev. Marie Trimble of Foursquare Church of Lynwood, and many others accompanied the team on several trips. Those who could not attend the conference showed their support with prayers, fasting, and finances. The expenses for the conferences were absorbed by CWM. Carolyn committed herself to bringing the team into the area, until there was a release from the Holy Spirit that the assignment was completed. She viewed coming to Philadelphia as planting seed for the up-building of the kingdom of God.

With the expansion of their ministry, Carolyn and Charles began to talk to me about relocating to California and working in the ministry. I had just finished at Jameson School of Ministry and Jameson Bible College and was the pastor of an inner city ministry in the heart of South Philadelphia. It was located around the corner from the 17th District Police Station, an area plagued with crime and drugs. I knew several of the families operating the sell of drugs in that community. Carolyn and I had played with them as children, turning on the fire hydrants in the hot summer trying to find some relief. We swam together at the Marian Anderson YMCA and stood in line at the Uptown Theater to see James Brown and Stevie Wonder.

I had a heart for our former playmates. How had their lives turned out so differently from mine? I felt an obligation to try and reach them with the gospel. It was time for me to move forward and it turned out to be good training. We partnered with the Philadelphia Archdiocese and ran a summer lunch program for economically disadvantaged children in the neighborhood. Alcoholism, drugs, and unemployment were rapid, as in any inner city. It was not unusual for me to walk into the bars along Point Breeze Avenue with my bottle of oil and pray for everyone in the bar. Those sitting at the bar stools would turn around together and announce, "Here she is," and then proceed to raise their hands so I could anoint them all with oil. I would walk up and down Point Breeze with a bull horn, and stand outside of the liquor stores and offer prayer to anyone who would accept it. My desire was to offer hope to those who felt hopeless and helpless.

One young woman I ministered to was the mother of two boys. She gave her heart to the Lord, right then and there, and began to make some decisions about her life. She eventually moved to Louisville, and now she and her husband pastor a church and an outreach ministry to ex-offenders and their families.

Prior to accepting Charles and Carolyn's invitation to join their ministry, I was linked into an organization that was a stepping stone in preparing me to be a "revolutionary" in the body of Christ. I was working for the National Headquarters of Opportunities Industrialization Centers of America (OIC). Dr. Sullivan started the OIC to "help others to help themselves." The organization, founded by the late Rev. Dr. Leon Sullivan, offered training to young adults and earned Rev. Dr. Sullivan the attention of the Rev. Dr. Martin Luther King, Jr. He also gained the respect of his colleagues, corporate executives, and politicians. He spearheaded the Selective Patronage Boycott. Dr. Sullivan led three hundred local ministers and their congregations; he inspired hundreds to "Don't buy where you don't work." Thanks to the success of the boycott, thousands of African Americans in the Philadelphia-Delaware Valley were able to get entry-level jobs in the banking, manufacturing, and retail industries. This allowed them to raise the socioeconomic status in their communities.

The New York Times featured the Selective Patronage Program with a front page story, and later, *Fortune* magazine brought the program to the attention of the nation. By 1962, the effectiveness of Dr. Sullivan's boycotts came to the attention of the Southern Christian Leadership Conference (SCLC) headed by Dr. Joseph Lowery. They persuaded Dr. Sullivan to share information with them on his success. The exchange led to the SCLC's economic arm, Operation Breadbasket, in 1967, headed by Jesse Jackson.

Before the recognition, achievements, awards, and board appointments, Rev. Dr. Sullivan was a husband, a father, and a man called of God. I believe his family paid a great price in sharing him with us and I thank them for the sacrifice. I saw, first hand, the sacrifices that are required of us to serve God. Rev. Dr. Leon Sullivan's family shared him with the world because of his purpose—to impact the way this nation and the world would be molded.

I say all this to drive home the point of how God uses us. Now, I'm not comparing Carolyn to those men and women who died fighting for civil rights. But, like Dr. Sullivan, Carolyn's family had to share her with the world as she fought principalities and exalted the kingdom of God.

During my last five years with the OIC, I traveled extensively across the country working in a technical assistance role to the executive directors and vocational staff. However, I was about to embark on a journey that I couldn't even imagine. It set the course for my life's work. After saying "yes" to Charles and Carolyn, I naively resigned from my job, sold my car, and all my household goods.

Initially, I thought I would live in California for a few years, put my time in as if I was in the Army, and then receive additional direction from God for my life later. I envisioned that I was doing the will of God, putting in my time to then be released and go on with my own life and ministry. I saw the whole thing as a short "tour of duty." I did not realize that I had signed up for a journey that included advanced training in spiritual warfare, confrontation with witches, intercession, praise and worship, administration, family, commitment, devotion, tears, submission, misunderstandings, healing, emotional and physical separation, divorce, missions, loss, gains, victory, rescue, salvation and restoration, sickness, and even death.

As I prepared myself to depart from Philadelphia, a few of my close friends threw me a farewell party. Strangely, in attendance were some people I had never even met before. Several of my friends considered me pretty radical in the way I chose to go about sharing my faith. Without my knowledge, they invited their friends from main-line denominations and traditional churches to my party. Their motive was that I'd pray for their friends to receive the baptism of the Holy Spirit.

I distinctly remember one couple. They were members of The Garden of Prayer Church of God In Christ, which had a rich history. It was founded by Elder Dabney and his wife, Mother E. J. Dabney. She was a female pioneer of great proportions for women in ministry. She authored the book,

"What it Means to Pray Through." It tells how she entered into a covenant of prayer with God for three years and people from around the world came to the church to receive prayer; signs and wonders followed the believer and the word of God. (Some years later, I shared the story of Mother Dabney's prayer life with Gloria Copeland; she asked me to send her a copy of the book.)

The husband had been saved for over twenty-five years and still desired the infilling of the Holy Spirit with the evidence of speaking in tongues. There were about twenty-three persons present in my friend's row house in the Mt. Airy section of Philadelphia, including people of the Baptist and Pentecostal faith. Some were believers who wanted to experience the power of the Holy Spirit. As we approached the end of the party we offered prayer to every person who desired to be filled with the Holy Spirit with the evidence of speaking in tongues as the Holy Spirit led. Our God is faithful to those who seek and ask; everyone received the infilling of the Holy Spirit including the husband of the Spirit-filled wife.

Before my journey to California, I went home to Virginia, to spend Christmas with my family and say goodbye. I explained to them that my move to California was to work with Carolyn in the ministry. That was really all the information I could give them, since it was the only information I had myself. Anyway, my lack of details was met with looks of suspicion. I could see my family collectively remembering my "BC" years (Before Christ). I could see them wondering, "What is she up to," and thinking, "Here we go again." It seemed to them that I was pulling another one of my crazy stunts only this time I was saying God was telling me to do it. I could tell they all wanted to be supportive, they just weren't sure if they should be.

So, there I was about to make a major leap of faith to relocate to California and work in ministry without any idea of what I would be doing, what the salary would be or benefits. I was about to enter what I considered an Abrahamic experience. I left what was familiar and embarked on a journey to an unknown land.

Carolyn and Peggy

Dickie

Chapter 5

Ministry Experience, Challenges, and Lessons

It was December 1983 when I finally moved to California. I was excited about being involved in full time ministry at Walnut Faith Center Church. The composition of the congregation was muti-culture. The ministry had also expanded in size and recognition.

As a visionary and a pioneer who was not afraid to follow the leading of the Holy Spirit, Carolyn had a confidence and a dependency upon God that set her apart. She was extremely professional in the manner in which she handled church affairs. Carolyn insisted on proper record keeping and had several notable accounting firms analyze the financial reports to make sure that we were meeting ethical and financial obligations. She expected no less than perfection from her staff, which now included me.

My initial welcome to the church was a good one. But as days grew into weeks, I began to experience opposition from some of the staff. They were accustomed to Carolyn or Charles telling them what to do and did not like that they now had to report to me, as Director of Church Operations. I considered myself mature enough to handle the challenges, but having no one to talk to about it was difficult. I considered myself as being loyal; the pastors had too much to do to deal with to be bothered with petty issues. I didn't expect to be shown any favoritism, nor would I have wanted it. I was there with the purpose of being a blessing, but I soon began to realize that neither undergraduate, graduate school, nor Bible college had prepared me for what I'd gotten myself into. I remember hearing Dr. C. M. Ward in an interview share from his book, "What Bible College Did Not Teach Me." He said how sometimes we think school has prepared us for some things only to find out that on the job training has its own hurdles, learning curves, dilemmas, battles, good times, and adventures.

At times, I thought, "Hey, I did not go to school for this. They need someone else; I didn't major in journalism or accounting." I can remember when I was given the assignment of preparing an ad for the Los Angeles Tribune. I had to do so many rewrites that I eventually lost count, but the experience turned me into a print ad expert! All the while I was thinking, "Where is the glamour of ministry?" If it wasn't newspaper ads, then I was boxing tapes, mailing envelopes, or a trillion other things. But, my commitment to God was stronger than any personal objections I may have experienced. I stayed confident that things were going to all work out for my good.

My responsibilities grew to include coordinating Covenant Women's Ministry and later, Daughter's of

Destiny Ministry. Every November, women from across the country would find their way to the conferences. Special guests included Donna Summers, Helen Baylor, the late Archie Dennis, the late Billy Preston, Candi Staton, Beau Williams, and many others. I started traveling with Carolyn on trips to minister the Word of God, as well. I was afforded the opportunity to meet several wonderful people including the late Archbishop Benson Idahosa of Nigeria, the late Lester Sumrall, the late Vicki Jamison-Peters, Richard and Lindsay Roberts, R. W. Schambach, Marilyn Hickey, Dr. Wanda Davis-Turner, and Bishop T. D. Jakes.

We traveled from the Rockies, to Albuquerque, to the Bible Belt; from the City of Brotherly Love, to Miami, from the Panhandle, to the Motor City, and from the Islands all the way to the Motherland. With each city and country we travelled to, we ministered at all kinds of churches and denominations. Needless to say, we were sometimes greeted with skepticism, but we knew God would show us how to speak to those we were visiting. We always joined hands in prayer and asked God to use Carolyn to deliver his Word to the people in such a way to glorify Him. By the time Carolyn was done ministering, she would not only have delivered a powerful life changing message but won the hearts of many who came into contact with her.

Life with Dr. Carolyn Harrell: A Magnanimous Journey

The Flyer for Carolyn's 1990 Women's Conference

Dr. Peggy R. Scott

The Flyer for Carolyn's
1994 Women's Conference

Life with Dr. Carolyn Harrell: A Magnanimous Journey

Special Guests at Carolyn's 50th Birthday Celebration
Beverly Hills Hotel, Beverly Hills, California;
Yolanda Adams, Billy Preston, Broderick Price,
Beau Williams, and Phil & Brenda Nichols

In retrospect, there were many lessons for me to learn. For instance, I can admit now that I was more than a little naïve. It has taken me a while to reach this resolve, but I can say it was all worth it. I purposed to do it as unto the Lord, to fulfill any and all that was entrusted in my hands. My intent and purpose for being there was to be a blessing, to help and not a hindrance. Like so many others in ministry, I had bought into the "Sold out to God" ideology. We traveled the world proclaiming "Jesus is Lord," and nothing was more important than that message. We were on a mission to do what God had called us to do; I believe, not realizing that we were sacrificing more than God required of us.

God created the family before the church. He was about relationship then, and is so now. There is a way to accomplish what God has called you to do without sacrificing your spouse, family, and children while on your way to heaven. I understand what it means when your family and friends reject you for your commitment to Christ and you take a stand for righteousness. In our family, as in many ministry families, there have been too many casualties while we were off saving the world. I acknowledge that the issue is great, but we must find ways to care for others without neglecting and hurting the ones we love. We must begin somewhere, to be open, transparent, and acknowledge our intentional and or unintentional mistakes. How many pastors' wives have become emotionally damaged while doing ministry? Seminars are beginning to address the concerns of pastors' wives, commonly referred to in some circles as "first ladies." Dr. Wanda Davis-Turner is one who has ministered and addresses many of the issues as they relate to pastors' wives.

As we have seen in recent years, whatever challenges we face in society; they are visible in the church too. It would be beneficial for more seminaries, schools of theology, leadership institutes, schools of helps, ministries and other organizations to prepare upcoming leaders by creating curriculums to address the family in ministry. Then, there is the issue that is unique to women who are successful in ministry and within their husband's. Let's bring it out in the open. There is a view and an opinion that some women are considered to be more anointed than their husbands and vice versa. Then there are some women whose finances are greater their spouses. It presents some challenges to the male and female ego. It is a misnomer and inaccurate faulty view about giftings and impartations. God is the one who determines and sets in the body the various gifts. Christ needs you to step forward to share, minister, and teach others. Teach how to preserve your family while fulfilling ministry. We know there has been and will continue to be a spiritual attack from the Enemy to destroy marriages and families. I believe it is the responsibility of the spouse who is in leadership position to lead by example. They should exemplify how the other spouse should be recognized, accepted, and esteemed. It is not uncommon to see. We can attest to situations where the husband (pastor) receives the attention and the wife is shuffled to the side, intentionally or unintentionally. What about the children who rebel because they feel the loss of one or both parents? I know some of you are deep and have a theological response on what to do and how to do it. However, I am encouraging you to address these issues with practical truths.

Although these insights were birthed out of some personal losses, the losses and gains have structured me into who I am today. I have exceeding joy! It was indeed a magnificent journey. It was a journey of steadfastness, preaching, teaching, and exercising of my faith. It molded and shaped me.

Life with Dr. Carolyn Harrell: A Magnanimous Journey

"You can't do anything about the length of your life, but you can do something about its width and depth."

Chapter 6

God's Cheerleader to the Body of Christ

By this time Carolyn was ministering and travelling throughout the continental United States and abroad and had begun making regular appearances on Trinity Broadcast Network (TBN). You don't travel the world ministering with Carolyn and not pick up a few stories along the way. Kitty, never met a stranger, which made for some interesting trips, to say the least.

On one trip, Carolyn met a couple who was being haunted. As we sat down with them, they began to share their concerns about demonic activity they believed was taking place in their home. According to the couple, after they went to bed they would be suddenly awakened by the television at the same time every night. They were always sure that they had turned the television off before going to bed, and they had become fearful that an unwelcomed spirit was operating in their home. Later, it was determined that the couple was neither haunted nor was there a demon inhabiting their home. The television was programmed to come on at a certain time. Turning off the timer solved the problem.

Then, there was the shooting we encountered while in Hampton, Virginia. While Carolyn's ministry was well known across the country and abroad, very few people knew of her in the southeastern part of our home state. During one of her rare visits to minister in Virginia, we were staying at a hotel and heard what seemed to be gunshots outside of our window. Instinctively, Kitty and I dove to the floor in an effort to avoid any stray bullets. After a few minutes we picked ourselves up off the floor and peered out of the window to see that a shootout is exactly what had occurred. A minister from Nevada was in an adjoining room and saw the entire ordeal; apparently, a drug deal had gone bad. Well, I became hysterical as I began to imagine that the gunmen were next door. I was insistent that I could hear them saying our room number. Carolyn tried to calm me down, reassuring me that there was no one outside our door. Actually, we had seen the police frisk some of the men and take them away in a police car. The ministry staff came to the hotel to check on us and offered to move us into another hotel.

On a trip with Marilyn Hickey to spread the gospel to the Aborigines in Australia, Carolyn was speaking at an open air meeting. There was one man, well known by all the villagers, who had climbed up into a tree. We assumed it was probably to get a better view of what was going on. As Carolyn began to share the gospel and her testimony of deliverance from alcoholism, the town witnessed the man, known as "the town drunk," climb down from the tree and give his heart to the Lord Jesus Christ.

On another occasion, a very well-known Word of Faith teacher wanted Carolyn to speak at Anaheim Convention Center and to specifically share the story about a relative who'd spit in her face as a young girl. Carolyn declined the offer to share about the spitting incident; her reply being, "I still have unsaved relatives that I want to win to the gospel." She shared intimate details about her life only when led by the Holy Spirit. In this situation she was convinced that it would be a possible hindrance to their salvation.

Then there was the time Carolyn had me "kidnap" the late Archbishop Idahosa. Well, "kidnap" may be too strong of a word. Archbishop Idahosa was travelling from the Pacific Islands and had a layover in Los Angeles. I was given instruction by Carolyn to meet his flight in Los Angeles and to persuade him to cancel his reservations at a hotel near the airport and convince him to come with me instead. I explained that we wanted to put him up in the Sheraton Hotel Industry Hills or the Shilo Inn, and we'd be honored if he would be our guest speaker on Sunday morning. He made it clear that he was tired from his travels, needed rest, and was not going to accept the invitation to minister Sunday morning at our church.

Archbishop Idahosa was a man of authority and strong willed, but so was Carolyn. I got on the phone with her and she told me to do whatever I had to in order to get him to accept our invitation. Well there I was in the middle of two

Life with Dr. Carolyn Harrell: A Magnanimous Journey

authoritative people, each insisting that I adhere to their agenda. Archbishop Idahosa had not met Carolyn, nor did he know me prior to my arrival at the airport. He directed us to take him to his original hotel and as the driver proceeded I continued to pray and use all the power of persuasion available to me. Finally, he relinquished and accepted our invitation. As a result, there followed many years of fellowship among our families and co-laboring in the gospel. We even supported the building of an elementary school in Benin City. Carolyn and Margaret Idahosa, now Archbishop Idahosa, declared their sisterhood to each other and she invited Carol to speak at the Women's Conference in Benin City, Nigeria.

I was elated when we took our first trip to Nigeria (I had taught black history and you cannot adequately do so without discussing the historical significance of African heritage). What we observed while there was educational and life changing. It affected my self-esteem, my personal view of God's divine plan for a nation, and its people.

Carolyn was scheduled to be one of the speakers, with Apostle Corletta Vaughn and Candi Staton, and Bishop Sandra Phillips Hayden in attendance. Everything was all planned and suddenly Carolyn became ill; she was nausea and unable to stand. No matter what we gave her nothing seemed to work. Prayers were rendered, but to no avail.

I was so disenchanted. I wanted Carolyn to share her message of hope with the thousands of women gathered in Benin City, Nigeria. As I went to my room I was accompanied by some Christian sisters from California, and members of the church. I expressed my dismay and stated something to the effect that I wished it was me who was sick instead of Carolyn. No sooner had I made that statement I became ill, fainted, and fell on the bed. One of the young ladies with us was a registered nurse (RN); she said that I appeared to turn green and she was searching for my pulse. Finally, I was revived.

Carolyn recovered and rendered a powerful message.

Thanks to the opportunities afforded us, Carolyn became an internationally known minister. No matter where we went, no one ever doubted that she had the Word of the Lord in her mouth. As the senior pastor of Word Harvest Worship Church (formerly Walnut Faith Center Church) the founder of Covenant Women's Ministries and Daughters of Destiny Life Changing Seminars, and a noted author, she was viewed by many of her colleagues as "God's Cheerleader to the Body of Christ." Carolyn was definitely a pioneer and trailblazer supporting gospel rappers (when it was frowned upon by many), the Original Gospel Gangsters, encouraging Christian comedian Broderick Rice to display his God given gift of humor, and cheering Phil and Brenda Nicholas on to continue to sing their love songs. Carolyn was unselfish; she was always encouraging and promoting others to pursue their dreams. She assisted in fulfilling those dreams, whenever possible. So many people had been a blessing to her that she wanted to do the same for others.

One of Carolyn's goals was to help women and children. In the eighties she started programs such as Women Off Welfare (W.O.W), Operation Take-back,

Superior Minds, and Superior Attitudes Learning Center. Many of the women and children exposed to the programs and Carolyn's empowerment teachings such as Glenda Lashley, Lea Morgan, and Carol Williams have successful careers today.

She became a frequent guest on TBN and highly sought after for conferences and retreats, but she managed to never let it all go to her head. Carolyn stayed the same down to earth person she'd always been, making friends with just about everyone she met.

Carolyn had the privilege of preaching the gospel in numerous pulpits. She ministered with veteran ministers Marilyn Hickey, Rev. Richard and Lindsay Roberts, Bishop T. D. Jakes, Bishop Dennis Leonard, Dr. Fred & Mrs. Betty Price, Rev. Kenneth & Gloria Copeland, the late Bishop Isaiah & Dr. Gloria Williams, Bishop Harold & Pastor Brenda Ray, Dr. John & Mrs. Diana Cherry, Rev. Shirley Caesar, Dr. Wanda Davis-Turner, Bishop Mark Chironna, Rev. Ed Dufresne, Evangelist Dwight Thompson, Dr. Myles Munroe, Apostle Corletta Vaughn, Dr. Bridget Hilliard, Apostle Ernest Leonard, Bishop Don Meares, Bishop Ernestine Reems, the late Archbishop Benson Idahosa, and many others. After hearing Carolyn preach, the late Rev. Oral Roberts gave her a compliment that Carolyn cherished for many years. Even songstress Yolanda Adams acknowledged Carolyn on one of her recording jackets for the impact Carolyn's messages made on her life. As she gave her testimony of her deliverance from alcohol, molestation, and family abuse, she often left those listening in awe of God's power. Anyone who knew Carolyn never forgot her.

I was happy to be a part of her achievements. There were some who were suspect of my motive, but I endured and persevered because of my love for Carolyn and my commitment to God. People with loved ones in ministry can understand the depth of what I am saying. You hurt when they hurt and you rejoice when they rejoice. There is nothing you will not do to make your loved ones' burden a little lighter. My salary was a modest one. It may be difficult to believe, but I never ever asked for or even borrowed money from Carolyn. Carolyn was a giver and it was not unusual for her to give gifts to me and many others.

During that time in our lives, God made everything so clear. He used all the hurt and the pain we had experienced as children to give us purpose. It was clear that we had a calling on our lives and I planned to stay the course. I came to discover and understand that the path I was traveling was a path of co-laboring and submission; a path of training orchestrated by God. We had weathered the storms of life and now we were enjoying the fruits of our labor. But, we would be tested, yet again. What happened next tore everything apart.

Life with Dr. Carolyn Harrell: A Magnanimous Journey

Carolyn was invited by Archbishop Idahosa to be his special guest at the foundation laying ceremony of Christian Faith University in Benin City, Nigeria

IDAHOSA WORLD OUTREACH

"Go ye into all the world, and preach the gospel" Mark 16:15

Most Rev. Prof. B. A. Idahosa
Archbishop

August 12, 1992

RECEIVED AUG 1 8 1992

Pastor Carolyn Harrell
Word Harvest Worship Center
1680 Keystone Ave.
Pamona, CA 91767

My Dearly Beloved,

LETTER OF INVITATION: BE MY SPECIAL GUEST AT THE FOUNDATION LAYING CEREMONY OF THE INSTITUTE OF CONTINUOUS LEARNING, CHRISTIAN FAITH UNIVERSITY.

Greetings in the name of our Lord and King, Jesus Christ.

Study to show yourself approved unto God, a workman that needeth not be ashamed, rightly dividing the word of truth.
II Timothy 2:15

This is to request your honored presence in our midst as MY SPECIAL GUEST to the Foundation Laying Ceremony of the Christian Faith University.

With gratitude to God, I will be 54 years old on September 11th, 1992. Of these years of my life so far spent, the Lord has used me in countless ways to give a helping hand to individuals, groups as well as the government of our land, in the furtherance of their goals.

The Lord God Almighty has seen the need for us to leave a solid legacy behind for our children, and so have I. The Lord has seen the need for our children to be properly brought up in the way they should go, so that when they are old, they will not depart from it; and so have I. I realize that it is easier to train up a child than to reform an adult.

Based on this burden given to me by God to leave a mark for generations yet unborn, the Church of God Mission International, Inc., in partnership with several of our friends and partners, want to build a university that will set an unprecedented pace in the annuals of our history.

HONOR US THEREFORE WITH YOUR PRESENCE ON THE 12TH OF SEPTEMBER 1992, AT 10:00 A.M., THE VENUE WILL BE THE UNIVERSITY SITE, -G. R. A., BENIN CITY, (some yards away from the Faith Miracle Center).

——————— International Headquarters ———————
P.O. Box 29400, Washington, D.C. 20017 (301) 779-4234

Chapter 7

When it All Falls Apart

It is often said that there is a cost for the anointing. As Christians we realize that we are not exempt from trials and tribulations simply because we are Christians. The Word of God says that if we suffer with Him we shall reign with Him. It was in 1991 that Carolyn's marriage to Charles unraveled publicly. The dissolution of a marriage always carries with it a "fallout," but you can't imagine the damage done when it affects not only your children and relatives, but your spiritual family as well. That was the case with Carolyn and Charles' divorce. I will refrain from sharing any accounts about the dissolution of the marriage other than how it impacted the lives of hundreds of people. I know we like to think that what we do, the decisions we make in life only affect us. That is a fallacy for all of us.

It didn't take very long for the religious community to become aware of Carolyn and Charles' separation. She was avoided by some as if she had a plague. The isolation, shunning, and lack of sympathy were devastating for Carolyn. In my opinion, she was treated by some as if it was something contagious, "...it happened to you; it can happen to me, so I am going to keep my distance from you." Many of the phone calls and invitations ceased; it was like Carolyn became a social outcast overnight. It was a difficult challenge for Carolyn. I saw the miraculous hand of God anoint her to minister to God's people only to see her recline in the bed or a chair afterwards to find solace as our mother read Scriptures to her, in much the way as David played music for Saul. How different it is today. Some people don't bat an eyelash when they hear about the failure of marriages of high profile individuals.

Eventually, people's attitudes and opinions toward Carolyn began to change when they found out the facts about the dissolution of the marriage. Carolyn did not want the termination of her nineteen year old marriage. Needless to say, the lives of her children were greatly affected.

As Carolyn's marriage was ending in divorce, I was facing my own private failure of a marriage. I married against God's will. I couldn't be there for Carolyn and handle my own loss at the same time; it was too much for me. Somehow, I had become entangled in Carolyn's web. Rumors about inappropriate behavior were shared with me, but I had dismissed them because I did not want to believe them. I later shared them with Carolyn after her marriage had officially ended and in her distress she lashed out at me. I said, "This is it!"

I would not assume blame for someone else's actions. I felt it was best for me to leave California. I packed my things and returned to Virginia to be with my extended family who loved me through every ordeal I had ever faced in life.

For a while Carolyn and I did not talk; I prayed about it and I knew she did also. The input of other people only inflamed the situation. It was important to me that Carolyn recover from her loss.

One day I received a phone call from Carolyn and she said, "Peggy I need you to come back to California to work in the ministry again."

My quick reply was, "Carolyn, I am not coming back to California [except] to visit."

Carolyn stated, "Peggy one thing I know about you is that all you need to know is that it is of God."

Within a month's time I had heard from God and I'd had several confirmations. I went back to California and resumed my ministerial and operations director position. We were together again.

Prior to their breakup, the church had been described as one of the fastest growing in California. But, that wasn't the case now. Amid swirling rumors, members weren't sure what was true and what was false. Several members left, some began their own ministries, while there were those who remained loyal to Carolyn and the ministry. In her emotional distress, Carolyn entered into another relationship that ended in an annulment.

In hindsight, I too was emotionally vulnerable. After my marriage had failed I experienced an additional personal trauma that I even omitted sharing with Carolyn. How do you admit to a brief encounter of inappropriate sexual advancements from a person in spiritual authority? I shared this information with a relative who initially did not believe me; however, later became convinced that I was telling the truth. As I reflect upon it, I was impressionable and vulnerable. I can only describe it as a black hole pulling me into a regrettable experience. How could I allow this to happen? The spirit of darkness preyed upon me but a greater Spirit and power set me free. Anyone who may have a similar experience, I pray for your complete deliverance and healing. Do not run any longer, or suffer in silence. Tell someone, even if it is a therapist or psychiatrist. I am not speaking as a victim, but as one who is free. My plea is that anyone involved, regardless of their role can find forgiveness and freedom.

Regardless of the chaos that had encroached Carolyn's life, she continued to serve as pastor of the church. Carolyn's speaking engagements had picked up again; she was in constant demand and was ready to move forward with life. When Carolyn was away I functioned as assistant pastor. While on the road, it was not unusual for Carolyn to send her entire honorarium to help with the church budget.

With things relatively back to normal, I began to travel with Carolyn again when I could. I remember one of our trips to TBN's Nashville studio. Carolyn became so sick during our layover in Dallas that we had to take her to the hospital and cancel the appearance. The incident was just a foreshadowing of things to come. Carolyn had already "paid the price for her anointing" through many trials and tribulations; but it seemed that the Enemy had launched an all out attack against her. She and her husband had divorced and yet that had just been the tip of the iceberg; there was a larger attack to come.

Life with Dr. Carolyn Harrell: A Magnanimous Journey

Carolyn, Dion and Corey

Carolyn and Tamika

Chapter 8

The Illness

Around 1997 Carolyn began to feel some challenges in her body. It had become difficult for her to walk or even stand. However, it wasn't until our mother died in September 1998 that Carolyn announced to the board that she would no longer be the pastor of Word Harvest Worship Church. Carolyn had a pastor's heart and wanted what was best for God's sheep. She knew that she could no longer function in that capacity, so she made the difficult decision to step down. Eventually, I moved back to my hometown.

Not too long after my return to Virginia, Carolyn moved to the Maryland–District Columbia area. Tamika had married a few years earlier and was living in Maryland with her husband and son. By the time Carolyn made the move back east, her health had declined considerably. In the meantime, Dr. John Cherry had become the official pastor of the church. Dr. John and Mrs. Dianna Cherry became very much involved in Carolyn's physical and spiritual care. They provided financial and medical support to Carolyn monthly. I will be forever grateful to them for their ministry of kindness.

Life with Dr. Carolyn Harrell: A Magnanimous Journey

Eventually, Tamika and her husband, Melvin, moved into Carolyn's home to help her with day to day care. I cannot say enough about Melvin's devotion. He cared for Carolyn as if she was his very own mother. I tried to remain supportive of Tamika as Carolyn's primary caretaker. My background in social work proved to be a tremendous help. It was not unusual for me to receive calls at any hour of the night from Carolyn and Tamika. Each one would call me frustrated with the other and with a different take on what was actually going on. I was there for them both emotionally, spiritually, and as frequent as possible physically.

A dear cousin, who Carolyn had been raised with, took her into her home in Virginia. Kitty relocated there as an effort to give Tamika and Melvin a respite. I was able to see Carolyn more often. Frequently, she requested that I come and have "church" with her, which she loved. She was extremely well taken care of by our cousin.

I vividly remember the last summer Carolyn and I were together as if it were yesterday. It was the summer of 2001. I was taking her out for an afternoon drive. We were going to Outer Banks, North Carolina about forty-five to sixty minutes from our birthplace, Chesapeake, Virginia. It was difficult seeing a person who was so full of life and joy; and now her body was racked with pain. She even needed assistance to walk. The trip was interrupted because of the pain and we had to return home.

The care of a loved one can be scrutinized and viewed differently, depending on who you are talking to. There is always some discussion about who is not helping and who is making the decisions. Carolyn wanted to stay in Virginia and simultaneously wanted to be with Tamika and her family. There was a tug-of-war going on, but I felt it was my role to be an intercessor and a supportive sister and aunt, but not an advisor regarding decisions about her children. By the time she left Virginia in mid August there was a rift between Tamika and the cousin who assumed the caregiver's responsibility. Initially, my cousin had accepted the responsibility of caring for Carolyn so Tamika could have a respite, but soon Carolyn was back in Maryland under Tamika's care.

Early on, I had identified my role as a counselor and peacemaker in the situation. Frequently, I received calls from some of Carolyn's friends saying that it was difficult to reach Carolyn by phone and that whenever they called they were told she was asleep or unable to come to the phone. Tamika had some concerns about how the medication made Carolyn feel and think; so she attempted to monitor her phone calls. I believe that she was doing the best that she could under some difficult circumstances; attempting to protect her mother's privacy. Those of you who knew Carolyn can be assured that she still found a way to make a few calls.

Carolyn and Tamika had different opinions on what was happening with her medical condition. I tried to remain supportive to both without showing partiality. I realized that it was a tremendous strain on Tamika. She had her own way of doing things, which were often different from what her mother desired. I can recall, several times, being on the phone with one and a call would come in from the other. I never let on. I tried to be there for both of them.

Those of you who were aware of Carolyn's condition, held on with hope and in faith that she would recover from the illness, but that was not the case. One of the most challenging moments for me was when Carolyn was hospitalized in Virginia. The side effects of the medication caused her to experience hallucinations. As real as the hallucinations appeared to her, it was still very painful for me to watch. It was not the quality of life Carolyn desired. I now believe she asked God to take her home.

I was devastated when I received a call from a relative saying that Carolyn's health had declined and they did not expect her to live. My immediate response was, "They do not know what they are talking about." Carolyn's physician had told us that her condition was not a life threatening disease. The calls kept coming. I decided to call Tamika to find out what was going on.

She acknowledged that the things I'd heard were true. She explained that she hadn't called because she didn't want to deal with the hysterics that might come from her mother's paternal relatives. My first reaction was to ask if she was including me in that group. She assured me that she wasn't, so I began making arrangements to travel to Maryland to see Kitty.

It was an absolutely painful and devastating experience for me when I made the trip through a torrential rain storm to Maryland and was not allowed to see Carolyn. As I came close to the freeway exit for Tamika's home, I called to confirm the right exit, only to be told by Melvin that Tamika was really upset and did not want any company. I did not see that coming and it was as if I had collided with an eighteen wheeler. I did not persist; thanks unto God that I'd had a friend drive with me to Maryland. We turned around and I literally cried all the way back to Virginia.

Earlier in September, Tamika had asked me to loan her and Melvin a substantial amount of money to take care of some bills. Fortunately, I was able to oblige. I had no intention of seeking repayment. I had learned from Carolyn to release that which you can without looking for it to be returned. This was only a few weeks prior to a conversation Tamika and I had about having a benefit for Carolyn. We discussed contacting some of Carolyn's friends in the music industry and having the event in Virginia. There weren't any indications at that time that Carolyn's health was on the decline, at least none that were shared with me. Tamika and I were getting along fine. There were no conflicts, no arguments, misunderstandings, or any conversations between us that suggested any problems in our aunt-niece relationship. Had there been some altercation or disagreement, then I could have had something with which to attribute her actions. I was utterly dismayed about not being informed of Carolyn's condition.

It was around December 16 and 17, 2002 that I began to receive calls inquiring about Carolyn's passing. My only response was that I had not been notified, but it could have very well been true. Many expressed that they knew how close Carolyn and I were, so of course they were surprised that I did not know about her death. My relatives in Virginia were frantic. They were understandably upset, as they did not understand why I didn't know about Kitty's death or funeral arrangements.

Through the years Carolyn had become estranged from our family in Virginia because of the distance. I began to encourage her to visit more often with our aunts, uncles, and cousins. Whenever she visited Virginia there was a feast and a celebration. Carolyn loved her family that she grew up with. It was difficult for the family not to have any details about Kitty's death.

We frantically searched the newspapers in the Washington, D.C. and Maryland area hoping to find any information. The calls kept coming in across the country from renown ministers of the gospel and lifetime friends wanting to know the arrangements. We had no information to share with them. I contacted local pastors in the Virginia-Maryland area who had visited Carolyn when she was sick, thinking maybe they had some information. They were as dismayed as I was.

Finally, Tamika did call one paternal aunt and left a brief message, after the funeral, announcing that Carolyn had passed away. I never received a call, and to this day I do not know why. I have never been able to understand what led to the change in our relationship. When word finally reached me, I was informed that a private funeral had already occurred; neither our father nor I were ever contacted to be in attendance. When Carolyn was ill our father drove down from Philly and visited with Carolyn several times. She remained in contact with him by telephone. I observed them in a father and daughter interaction that I had not seen for years. One or more individuals may not have wanted them to have a relationship. At that time, during the illness, she seemed to need him to be in her life.

I decided that my family would have a memorial service for Carolyn at our grandfather's home church (New Mt. Olive Methodist Church in Chesapeake, Virginia). My paternal grandfather and grandmother helped to raise Carolyn as a young child. It was the church she had grown up in. As the calls from Carolyn's colleagues continued to flood in, I shared with them my plans to hold a memorial service. Dr. Wanda Davis-Turner and Bishop Leo Lewis both rushed to my side and provided support to me and the entire family.

Although Carolyn was adored by our family, several relatives refused to attend the memorial. They could not get their minds around the fact that Carolyn's body would not be there to view, and felt that it would not provide them with any closure. For those in attendance it was our opportunity to celebrate her life. Another memorial service was held at From the Heart Church Ministries in Pomona, California—the former location of Word Harvest Worship Center Church.

There were so many stories circulating about the privacy and lack of announcing her death publicly. I think people could easily accept a private funeral, but the secrecy and not announcing her death to family, friends, and people who financially supported her was heartbreaking. It was presented as though that was Carolyn's desire. My response is, "I do not know; she never discussed it with me, nor did she have to." Even to this very day, I have never inquired as to why it happened the way it did. In my opinion, it does not change anything. The reason I am sharing this with you is to clear up some rumors. My position regarding the matter has always been that Carolyn is no longer in pain and is in the presence of the Lord.

My attitude towards Carolyn's children was one of sympathy and concern; they had just lost their mother, their best friend. I began to pray and intercede for Tamika. I reminded myself that Carolyn was counting on me to pray Tamika through any emotional pain. Having a background in social work helped me tremendously to understand the distress that care-givers often experience and how medication can influence not only the physical but also the mental and emotional health of the infirmed. I entered into a commitment to pray for Tamika with a relentless, persevering attitude for her emotional healing and restoration. I knew nothing about Tamika's own health challenge that was disclosed to me later.

Dr. Peggy R. Scott

Carolyn, Tamika, and Ernestine Sweet

Tamika

Life with Dr. Carolyn Harrell: A Magnanimous Journey

Chapter 9

Restoration

I kept up my vigil of prayer for Tamika, Dion, and Corey. My assignment was to keep the prayer wheel turning for them. In 2004, I received a telephone call from Tamika. She expressed that she had been dreaming about me and wanted to see me. I assured her that I would love for her, Melvin, and the boys to come and visit. That began the restoring of our relationship.

When they came for their first visit, I prepared one of her and Melvin's favorite southern dishes and enjoyed playing with their boys, Jordan and Christopher. Melvin shared with me much later that Tamika had shared her dreams with him and he'd encouraged her to call me. She was reluctant, since all contact with me had ceased, but Melvin had assured her, "Aunt Peggy is not going to turn you away."

During our conversations, I mostly listened. Offering replies would not have been productive and definitely wouldn't have changed anything. Tamika attempted to explain some of the reasons for her decisions. She felt that she was carrying out her mother's wishes. During times of sickness and loss, people are vulnerable to their caregivers and are often influenced by their beliefs and opinions. Unless there is someone available with godly counsel, one can be easily persuaded by the opinion of others. I will go on record to say that Carolyn was greatly loved and admired by many. Several, who were close to her and provided service and financial support during her years of illness, were not given the opportunity to say their goodbyes. When one has a regard for godly counsel through a pastor or minister of the gospel then one can openly receive impartial advice. However, if there is no regard you lean to your own understanding to make decisions. They are made from the flesh based upon strife or emotional wounds. To them, their actions are justified.

    Tamika and I began to visit one another fairly regularly and kept in contact. Tamika shared with me her battle with breast cancer, which resulted in a mastectomy. She remained in her physician's care and entrusted her health and future to the Lord. According to Tamika, she had renewed her relationship with the Lord. She wanted to live and help her husband raise their two young boys. One day, I received a call from Tamika after a visit from her physician; the latest tests revealed a tumor in her brain. Her doctor had scheduled an operation. She wanted me to be there with her and Melvin. I arrived and we spent time together; she had a smile on her face when she went into the operating room. When she came out of surgery that same smile was there. None of her motor skills were affected and we continued to place our hope in God. Jordan was nine years old and mature enough to be aware of what was going on. He was an independent fellow who had a very close bond with his mother.

Christopher was too young to understand all that was taking place. After a few months, another report from the physician indicated that the cancer had invaded Tamika's bones. There was nothing else the medical staff could do. It was at this time that Tamika and I had long talks about her desires for Jordan and Christopher. She wanted them to have an educational plan and for them to be raised in the church. Tamika went to the extent of drawing up legal papers. Should anything happen to her and Melvin, she wanted the boys to live with me.

Some relatives became disturbed by Tamika's decisions, but I refused to become a part of their squabbling. My focus was on making Tamika comfortable and carrying out her wishes. We would bring the boys to the hospital and have pizza parties in her room. One of my most difficult times was when I watched Tamika explain to her sons how much she loved them. She drew both of her boys close to her, looked them in the eyes, and with all the love of a mother told them how much she and Melvin loved them. She went on to tell them that she was sick and may not make it. She wanted them to know that she would always be with them, and their daddy would be with them. Aunt Peggy would always be there for them, too. She said, "If I do make it, then we are all going to go to Great Wolf Lodge" (an amusement park) in Williamsburg, Virginia. Children, being children, cheered!

Dr. Peggy R. Scott

Tamika and Melvin Evans' Wedding
Beverly Hotel

Christopher and Jordan Evans
Carolyn's Grandchildren

Life with Dr. Carolyn Harrell: A Magnanimous Journey

Christopher and Jordan Evans

The next day, Tamika asked me to take the children with me to Virginia. The hospital was in the process of identifying a hospice for her. Every day she seemed to get weaker and weaker. I called her brothers Dion and Corey and told them that they should come and visit their sister, now. Melvin contacted Charles and he talked with Tamika and me. I had not talked to Charles since the early 90's. He asked Melvin to find out if I would accept his call. His invitation was so graceful, I gladly accepted his call. It was as if nothing had ever happened. I could sense his genuine love and care for Tamika. After all, he was the "father" who raised her from the age of three.

During this time, Tamika left no rock unturned; she asked me to contact Dr. John and Mrs. Diana Cherry, so she could talk with them. Dr. Cherry was Carolyn's pastor and he and Mrs. Cherry displayed great acts of kindness to Carolyn during her illness. Dr. Cherry stepped in and established a pastor for the former Word Harvest Worship Church when Carolyn could no longer assume the responsibilities. Because Carolyn had given so much of herself to the "church" it may have been difficult for her children to understand the dissolution of the church, and the legal and ethical ramifications that went along with it. From their view point, she'd given her life to it and then it was gone. A church is a living organism, composed of a body of believers. The building is not the church. The people make up the church that is housed in a building, which is consecrated to do the work of the ministry. The building is real estate and the church is a corporation. The church belongs to God. In hindsight, some decisions made by Carolyn probably could have been done differently.

If there is one appeal that can be made to every pastor it is this: please do not sacrifice your family in the name of success of ministry. True success is obeying God while keeping your family intact.

On one hand you cannot be too lenient with your family and over indulgent, but on the other hand you cannot ignore them because it is "you and God against the world." There has to be a balance. There is wisdom available from God for us to function in a way that brings Him glory and honor. Sold out does not mean an abandonment of your responsibilities as a husband, wife, or parent.

God desires our obedience and the denying of self. Whenever there is a denying of self, we have the best interest of others in mind and not ourselves.

One of my last evenings with Tamika, she called me close and whispered in a low voice, "Aunt Peggy I have something that belongs to you and I've had it for six years." Carolyn had told me before her death that she had told Tamika to give a certain item to me, but she knew she was not going to do it. I told Carolyn that it was all right. She had been a wonderful sister to me and our relationship was not about things. Tamika went on, divulging the conversation she'd had with her mother, not knowing that I already knew about the situation years ago.

I listened carefully as she said, "I have something that belongs to you and I want you to have it today, take it with you today. It's yours." My response was, "Thank you, Tamika.

She replied, "Oh, Aunt Peggy, this is nothing for you to say thanks to me."

You will never know the spiritual impact that had on me. It wasn't the value of the possession, but the spiritual significance. It showed what was in Tamika's heart in regards to me. I always considered Tamika as a daughter; the three of us shared many experiences—ups and downs. I saw the anger and unforgiveness that Tamika had toward others dissipate. On one occasion, during a hospital visit she said, "Aunt Peggy, I have tried to make it right with everyone."

Tamika wanted to spare the boys and gave me very specific instructions on what to do. I took Jordan and Christopher home with me. They had spent the summer of 2007 with me and they loved being with their Aunt Peggy. It was now March 2008, and it happened to coincide with the Easter holiday and Spring Break. Sometime between 8:00 a.m. and 8:30 a.m. on March 29, Good Friday, Melvin called so the boys and I could talk to their mother. She was in hospice and literally unable to speak, so he put the telephone to her ear so she could hear us on the phone. I left home for an appointment about 8:35 a.m. By 8:45 a.m. I received a phone call that Tamika had passed.

Melvin rushed from Baltimore to Virginia to be with his boys. I will never forget the look on Jordan's face and how he clung to his dad. The little man that he is, he said, "Aunt Peggy, it's too early."

Melvin and I proceeded to make plans for the funeral according to Tamika's desires. She gave me the instructions to have a funeral for Melvin's benefit. Tamika felt that he needed it. She also requested that I give the eulogy and consented to have the funeral at From the Heart Church in Maryland, followed by the cremation of her body. Unfortunately, Tamika's brothers (Dion and Corey) declined to attend the funeral due to where it was held.

While Tamika had resolved certain issues, it was clear that they had not. I believe they were still struggling with issues regarding the latter part of Carolyn's life. Unlike Tamika, they weren't ready to forgive, yet. Discord, when left unattended, can contaminate others. It was time for me to pull out the prayer wheel again and set up a prayer vigil for my sister's two sons.

I began to call their names before the Lord, and about four months later I received a phone call from Carolyn's eldest son, Dion. He apologized for his behavior towards me. He confessed that he had not been a good nephew, but declared his intentions to do better. I was so happy to hear from him, and not just for the apology he gave. I was excited to hear about Dion renewing his commitment to the Lord. He was reading his Bible and seeking help from God in certain areas of his life. A little later, I heard from Corey. God is faithful!

Epilogue

In September 2009, the Holy Spirit led me to have a Summit in California called, "A Time to Remember Dr. Carolyn Harrell." Initially, it was planned as an intimate dinner for a few colleagues, former church members, friends and family. Well it ballooned into a wonderful experience; the presence of the Holy Spirit was evident. There were those in attendance who were former members of WHWC, but who are now serving in the fivefold ministry. There were men and women present who were impacted and inspired by Carolyn's preaching of the gospel and are now serving as educators, city officials, and executives of corporate companies.

Where do I begin and how do I share with you my most intimate thoughts about missing someone who was so well loved by so many? Not a year since her death have I not met someone who did not know Carolyn had passed away. It is eight years later and there are some who are only now hearing of her passing. Just recently I was contacted via email by someone wanting to know, "Whatever happened to Carolyn Harrell? Where is she, and why have we not heard from her in a long time?"

I guess one of the reasons I am writing this book about my journey with Carolyn is because it taught me the practical things in life and how to live them. It's easy to go to church every Sunday and read the Bible—to know the principles of how God wants us to live our lives. But, it is quite another thing to actually do it.

Carolyn was one of those rare people who led by example. She taught me how to be a good sister, a good aunt, a good daughter, and a good minister. I was taught so many practical principles for living from her—what to do, as well as what not to do. Most importantly I learned forgiveness. Without that one simple principle, I can't even imagine how my life would have turned out.

What is my life like without my beloved sister? It is so much different than I imagined. We used to sit around and joke about what we were going to do together in our senior years. Carolyn and I always joked that in our sixties we were going to be like the Delaney Sisters.

There is probably not a message preached that does not make reference to something she taught me. She was so real…so genuine, and wanted the best for anyone who came into her life. I know several now prominent singers, motivational speakers, and preachers that she reached out to and encouraged before anybody knew them on a national scale. She would take the clothes off her back, the rings off her fingers, the shoes off her feet, and give them away. Oh! Indeed she was a saint because she was a child of God. She was not perfect, but forgiven, as we all are.

I have no doubts about her commitment to the welfare and wellbeing of God's sheep and her love for her three children. Carolyn loved her family greatly, her beloved daughter, the late Tamika Evans, eldest son, Dion, youngest son, Corey; and grandchildren, Jordan, Christopher, Cameron, and Carrington.

Her contributions to the body of Christ must not die but live on. Carolyn lives on through the lives of every person she touched, every member of Walnut Faith Center, Word Harvest Worship Church, and the body of Christ at large. She was a jewel and is greatly missed. Today, it is not uncommon to hear prominent men and women of the gospel reflecting the treasures and nuggets Carolyn preached years ago. She tapped into the Spirit of God's treasure chest and these spiritual insights continue to be relevant. We continue to pay tribute and honor to the gift God shared with us, by continuing to be servants in the kingdom of God.

The celebration of Carolyn's life did not occur as one would expect. However, seven years later, the Spirit of God laid it upon my heart to share our story. The Holy Spirit was saying that now is the time to speak up, to answer some questions, to share some of the trials and triumphs of an ordinary girl who had a big heart…an ordinary girl who believed that she could make a difference. She lives on in you and me because God stamped and imprinted his servant in our hearts.

Some people you meet and forget their names. Others you meet and you never forget them. I believe Carolyn was such a person. It was not her doing, but the working of an Almighty God. To Him belongs all honor, glory, power, and dominion.

Carolyn,

Thanks for the Memories . . .

I remember Carolyn:

When I think of Carolyn Harrell and her *"Legacy of Love,"* I think of the word *"Friend"* — *a valued person, united in the same purpose."* Carolyn and I definitely shared the same purpose: *Our love for God...Our love for His Word...Our love for souls!*

A smile comes to my face as I recall, with excitement, the memories I have of her. I know our friendship was a divine connection!

Carolyn had charisma to burn, and a natural ability to uplift everyone around her. We traveled to many conferences and crusades across the country and she was always such an encourager for my husband, myself, and the evangelistic ministry God has entrusted to us for the past 46 years.

One night, as we arrived into Ontario, California on a late flight, she said, *"Zo, I'll just take you home, and spend the night at your house."*

We hopped into her Rolls Royce and journeyed down Interstate 15. Suddenly, with absolutely no warning, the car started shaking and swerving back and forth across the freeway! Cars were flying around us. Something was terribly wrong, and it had happened so fast we couldn't comprehend what was going on! But when you know God, you just start calling out to Him for HELP!!!

Carolyn and I were both calling out to God for *our* protection, as well as those flying down the CA freeway around us, going 70 mph or faster. We were praying for safety to get to the shoulder of the road, *which was 3 lanes over to the right.* We were asking for guidance to get the *out-of-control* car over to the shoulder and to a complete stop! It was really a miracle that no one was hurt, and not a scratch on the car. Our angels made a way where the situation looked impossible.

When we were able to get the car stopped, with our hearts beating very fast, we realized our tire had blown out. To make a long story short, Carolyn was able to call her son, Dion, for help. When he arrived and looked at what had happened to the car, he came to the passenger's side, stuck his head in the window and said, *"Mom… This is nothing but the devil!"* He removed what was left of the shredded tire, helped us with the spare, and we went on our way.

I looked at Carolyn and said, *"You know, girlfriend, if we had been in my Ford (SUV), this would never have happened (smile)"* I can hear her laugh right now… and her laugh was so contagious!

As we safely made it home, Carolyn said, *"Zo, (with her uplifting, enthusiastic, vibrant joyfulness… and giving Satan no place) we must always remember… we have to hang on to our joy when the storms come!"*

The last time I spoke with Carolyn was weeks before her *"home-going."* Her voice and body were weak, but she still possessed a tremendous inner-strength in her faith because Carolyn was a woman who knew her God! She was a woman of confidence, focus, and passion. She possessed a great source of strength and inspiration, and she modeled joy in the midst of tremendous obstacles.

Dr. Peggy R. Scott

It is not always about what a person says, but what the person lives that says the most about their character. Carolyn modeled her faith in the midst of overwhelming private needs, with beliefs and Godly choices that made her strong, and she managed heartache and happiness with poise and grace.

I miss you Carolyn! But, I know that you are not only in my past... but in my future!

Lovingly,

~Zonelle Thompson
Dwight Thompson Ministries
P. O. Box 2202 Corona, CA 92878
www.dwightthompson.org

I remember Carolyn:

Carolyn Harrell was a great friend and had a wonderful ministry.

~Dr. Betty Price
Crenshaw Christian Center
Apostle Frederick K. C. Price, Senior Pastor
7901 S. Vermont Ave., L.A., CA 90044
www.faithdome.org

I remember Carolyn:

I have four stories about my best friend, Carolyn Harrell, that I think exemplify that type of person she really was.

"A friend loveth at all times, and a brother is born for adversity."~ Proverbs 17:17

Story One

Rarely do women meet one another and discover that God has intended them to walk as sisters/friends forever and forever. Such was my relationship with Dr. Carolyn Harrell. We met in the early 80's and though we were not in each other's homes every day, nor did we speak on the phone every day, God connected us by His Holy Spirit and love. No matter how much time elapsed between calls, every time we talked it was like we had just spoken the day before. Carolyn was a powerful woman of faith and charity. She not only would walk with you in faith, but she also put her faith into action. Case in point:

Bishop Wayne S. Davis and I purchased a bank and renovated it to become our new church. We told Dr. Carolyn and she was so excited. Taking time out of her schedule, she came down to do a walk-through of the building and pronounced miracles and blessings over our new vision. Two or three days later she called and said, "The Lord told me to call you. What else do ya'll need for your Church Opening Celebration?" Bishop Wayne replied, "$30,000 for the balance on the new pews."

Two hours later, a Mercedes pulled up to our home and Dr. Carolyn stepped out. She handed Bishop and I a check for $30,000 and told us, "Go pick up your pews."

She came to the opening and never mentioned that she let us have the money to buy the pews—not even when she made opening remarks. I loved that about her...she would give secretly and let the Lord reward her openly.

Story Two

During a very dark season of my life, I was scheduled to preach for the first time at Rev. James Cleveland's Women's Conference. Under much attack for accepting the invitation, it seemed the very powers of hell had risen up against me and my family.

On the afternoon I was to preach, one of my daughter's, in a moment of desperation, attempted suicide. While the limo drove me to the conference, the ambulance drove my husband and daughter to Daniel Freeman Hospital in Inglewood. The hardest assignment was for me to stand in that pulpit and preach to hundreds of hurting women, while hurting myself.

I called Pastor Carolyn and told her what happened. After praying with me, she said she would come to Los Angeles. I finished preaching that night and rushed to the hospital where my daughter was receiving treatment. In the middle of the night we were finally able to take her home. Early that morning, Dr. Carolyn Harrell arrived. She put us out of my daughter's bedroom and laid on the floor crying out to God for my daughter's life.

She ministered to her, to me, and to my husband. She sent for food to be brought to our home, and then she jumped back in her car to handle the busy life she led as one of God's most powerful pastors in the kingdom with her husband, Dr. Charles.

Story Three

Five or six years later, my same daughter was preparing to marry her high school sweetheart. This was the year my husband, Bishop Wayne S. Davis was sick and dying. Because of financial stress, spiritual warfare, and so many attacks on our personal and spiritual lives, I told Dr. Carolyn I was going to down-size the wedding for my daughter. I explained it would be nice, but simple.

She yelled over the phone, "The devil is a lie, this is a good girl who loves the Lord and she's marrying a fine, saved young man. So, before we downsize we upgrade."

I said "Carolyn, what will I do for money?"

She replied, "Shut Up...God will provide."

She had her office call and inform me that she was giving, as a gift, a horse driven carriage for my daughter and her groom to ride from the church, around the city and back to the reception in Inglewood. I was floored and my daughter was so encouraged and blessed. Every time I look at those photos of that precious young couple in that horse drawn carriage...I hear Carolyn's voice, "Shut Up...God will provide."

Story Four

After my husband died, I shared with Carolyn that I was alone, lonely, and even scared at times. She replied, "You just need to go out on a date!"

"A date," I thought, "with who?" I wondered, "As a lady you're not supposed to walk up to a man and ask him to dinner, are you?"

Three days later, Carolyn called and told me, "Dress up and get your hair styled. A limo will pick you up and then pick up a gentleman that I set up to go with you to Pomona, where the three of us will go to dinner."

She planned the entire night—limo ride, dinner, and picked the guy for me. That night was the beginning of a wonderful relationship with that gentleman.

Carolyn was a real sister/friend. I miss her so very much. In fact, five years ago while going through a tough divorce, my daughters and I laughed and said, "If Auntie Carolyn was alive...Mama you wouldn't be going through this. She would be kicking butt, preaching, and praying until things changed." We laughed just at the thought of things she would have done and said.

She often told me, "Wanda, you better pray that Kitty don't come out. I ain't always been saved!"

Even to this very day, when things get rough and I wish for the presence of my dear, precious friend...I laugh when I hear her voice "Pray Kitty don't come out!"

May these stories bless you and show you the Carolyn I knew and loved.

Carolyn was a true friend to me. I love her dearly and am often reminded of the things she said. It was Dr. Carolyn who told me, "Wanda, always be careful of what you sow, for you must reap what you sow. For what some people sow, they better pray for crop failure!" When I am tempted to do something wrong...I hear those words.

~Dr. Wanda Davis
Dr. Wanda A. Turner Ministries, Inc.
3695 F. Cascade Road
PMB 224 Atlanta, GA 30331
www.justwanda.org

Dr. Peggy R. Scott

I remember Carolyn:

Pastor Carolyn was a pioneer thinker. She was the first to actually conduct beauty seminars for born again women. She taught women that it was just as important to be beautiful outside as inside. She liberated me. Through her teaching, I had faith enough to get my first fashion art director position at Bullock's Department Stores. The first fashion show I ever produced was for her.

Though Tamika was twice my junior, she had a special bond with my sister Mal and me. We were able to remain with Tamika during her time of passing in hospice. I have a good report as the Lord allowed me to see the glory glow on her face one night. I will remember it as long as I live.

God blessed me to spend a weekend with Pastor Carolyn a few months prior to her passing. I cherish the sincere truths and affection she shared with me and my friend Charlayne at that time. I remember that even though she was in a wheelchair, she managed to pull it off with class and glamour in her mink coat and throw. She is probably up there in heaven glamming-up the angels! I miss them both.

~Paulette Whitfield Black
Publisher, Coverings Fashion Magazine
www.coveringsmagazine.com
coverings@coveringsmagazine.com

I remember Carolyn:

Dr. Carolyn Harrell was a great woman of God and a dear personal friend. I am mindful of an old Arabic saying:

> *If I had two loaves of bread,*
> *I would sell one for hyacinths*
> *For they would feed my soul.*

There are many things I want to say about Carolyn. First and foremost is that Carolyn loved God. She loved life and knew the importance of the truth. She knew that man doesn't live by bread alone. She was a woman who knew the value of feeding her soul and cherishing the joy and beauty of her journey with God. She certainly didn't lack for the earthly blessings that come with the favor of God. However, her being radiated the reality that life consisted in far more than what material blessings could offer. She knew how to purchase the hyacinths that fed her at the deepest place.

Because Carolyn was so devoted to God, she was devoted to empowering the people of God and expanding their experience of God. She wanted the people of God to invite the presence and power of God into their lives, and be more appreciative of it. She wanted them to be continually receptive to His voice. She wanted them to be able to access the gateway of His grace and to experience what "the old songwriter" said about the Holy Spirit when he called Him "the Spirit of great surprise." That was Carolyn's motivation and her way of being, both in personal life and in her calling in the body of Christ. Her passionate commitment to serving God and serving all those God sent her way, including me, was revealed in her deep nurturing presence and influence, her supreme ability to communicate and powerfully articulate and minister the Word of God, and her profound sensitivity to the Holy Spirit. That sensitivity enabled her to operate at deeper levels of the prophetic in the lives of people. The secrets of their hearts were not only revealed as she prophesied, but there were more clearly understood. She had an amazing ability to motivate us to reach for greater dimensions of faith and expression in our own destiny in and with God. My life was changed because of Carolyn's preaching and her prophetic utterances over me.

I think it is important to also acknowledge that Carolyn trusted God, even in the toughest times. Because she trusted in God, she had this way about her that made it seem as if she traveled light. What I mean by that is that she enjoyed the journey. She had an incredible ability to maintain a sense of humor and joy in the midst of challenges, setbacks, and change. She found a way to transcend things that would cause others to perhaps give up or quit. She fought the good fight of faith and her heart never wavered in that fight.

While there are so many other things that could be said about Carolyn, I want to say in closing that Carolyn was always relevant to the times she was in and to everyone she touched. Carolyn was everybody's friend no matter what generation you belonged to—young, old, or in-between. She connected to every stage and level of life. She went out of her way to make sure you felt loved, valued, and celebrated. She stirred the fire in all of our hearts and souls.

I miss her dearly, as I know you do. I look forward to that day, that great day of reunion when all the saints will be together again in sweet communion around the throne. She is already there waiting for us. I am sure that even as she made an impact on earth, she is making her impact on heaven.

I love and miss you Carolyn,

~Bishop Mark J. Chironna, PhD
The Master's Touch International Church
Orlando, Florida
www.markchironna.com

I remember Carolyn:

Back in the early days of women of faith conferences I saw a conference ad in Charisma magazine. I had not attended one before, but for some reason I was determined to go to this one. It was being held in Philadelphia and I did not want to go alone. So I was able to persuade someone to accompany me. Though the church refused to pay for the trip, I still could not deny the excitement I felt about this conference. I couldn't wait to get there. You would have thought that I knew the speakers, but I did not.

When we arrived at the conference I saw something that I had never seen before and will never forget. The group of women leading the conference were bold and powerful. There was one in particular who stood out. Her name was Carolyn Harrell. Not only did she minister in a new, bold way, but she made me feel like I was her "best friend." I don't know how she did it, but it felt as though I had known her all of my life. Because of Carolyn the Holy Spirit spoke to me and said, "You can do this same thing at home." He used Carolyn to give me the boldness to organize the women's conferences that my husband, Bishop E.L. Warren and I host every year. The interesting thing is that I never even met her!

~Ella Warren
Cathedral of Worship
Pastor E. L. Warren
215 N. 25th Street, P.O. Box 831, Quincy, IL 62306
1-800-453-6712
www.cow-elw.com

I remember Carolyn:

When I first met Dr. Carolyn Harrell she was really young. Immediately, I noticed the anointing upon her life and her sincere love for God. God caused us to come together. The way He used and was working through her was very evident. She would minister at my church, Center of Hope, and I would minister at her church. Because of her extraordinary and reckless faith, God did unusual and mighty things for Carolyn. She was very gifted in the prophetic word and deliverances. God used her to bring other people into the kingdom. She encouraged me so…it would build my faith.

~Bishop Ernestine Cleveland Reems
Founder & Senior Pastor,
Center of Hope Community Church
Oakland, CA
(510) 562-633-5145
Contact person: annleegrant22@yahoo.com

***

I remember Carolyn:

I had the opportunity to serve as an administrator and in other ministry support roles at Walnut Faith Center, which subsequently became Word Harvest Worship Church in Pomona, California where Dr. Harrell was the Senior Pastor. I got to know her personally. She was not only my pastor and employer, but also a spiritual mother, friend, and mentor. She taught the women that each one of us was uniquely created and designed by God. She encouraged the women to appreciate the uniqueness of their individual beauty and that every woman is a "designer's special." She encouraged and inspired me, my daughter, Anasa, and many women all over the world to use their God given authority. She pushed us to walk in our destiny, fulfill our God given purpose, become "agents of change", and to empower others. Many women (and men) embraced the principles that were taught and demonstrated by Dr. Harrell, and their lives are richer and more effective because of her influence, warmth, and "spirit of excellence."

Dr. Harrell inspired me to complete my higher education, and at one of the most crucial moments in her life when she was "fighting" to regain her own health, Dr. Harrell returned to California to attend my graduation ceremony at the University of LaVerne. When I saw her, she said, "Carol, I would not miss this for anything in the world." You have truly made my heart glad.

Not only will you get this degree but other degrees will follow! Don't be afraid to move out on your dreams and ideas, because those ideas will generate the wealth that is destined for you. Carol, you are a daughter of destiny."

Today, I am an accountant for one of the local municipalities and I am an adjunct professor in the School of Business and Applied Technology at Chaffey Community College. I have given empowerment and motivational messages to women in conference and workshop settings. Most recently, I signed a press release to announce my first "technology-based" invention. Not only did she speak "prophetically" into my life, but she spoke about the destinies of my daughter, Anasa, and my two grandsons, Randon and Mylon. What else can I say? I am still reaping the benefits from her "short time" here on earth; it has extended to generations within my own family.

Dr. Carolyn L. Harrell was a beautiful person. She is truly my inspiration and she will always be an inspiration to many others.

I have had the honor of having some wonderful women in my life who have nurtured me into the woman that I am today. My spiritual mother, the late Pastor Carolyn Harrell, was one of those women.

~Carol Williams
Adjunct Professor Chaffey Community College
City of Ontario, CA

I remember Carolyn:

There are so many memories that I can recall of how Pastor Carolyn impacted my life. One of the greatest was how she believed in me when I didn't believe in myself. She would always say, "There is greatness inside of you, Girl!"

During that time I was a hot mess! I was a young girl going through a divorce and raising two daughters as a single mother. I knew deep down that God would see me through, but every day was a struggle. One day Pastor Carolyn sat me down and asked me what was I going to do with my life. Needless to say, I didn't have a clue. She told me that I needed to go to school, get a degree and make something of myself. She said," ...Then you won't have to depend on no one, but God!" With all I was going through, I just could not see how school would fit in.

Eventually, I took her advice and enrolled in school. It was one of the most proud moments of my life. As the years passed and it was getting near to my graduation, I could hear Pastor Carolyn's words. I could not wait to tell her of my accomplishments and had hoped that she would be in attendance at my graduation. She was unable to make it due to her not feeling well, but she called me and told me how proud she was of me and how much she loved me! All I could do was cry tears of joy.

I have since remarried and have two handsome stepsons. My two little girls have grown and become beautiful little ladies. My degree has opened many doors for me in my career and I am so happy that I listened to Pastor Carolyn. I am so grateful that she saw me, even in my rough stages, but knew that I was a diamond in the rough.

I only wish she were still here to see some of the results of her labor of love and prayers for me. She never gave up on me and didn't hesitate to openly correct me when I needed it... just like a mother would. I often wish I could hug her, thank her and say to her, "Look what the Lord has done! I did it Pastor Carolyn, I did it!"…and sing her favorite song…I've been through the storm and the rain, but I made it. I had so many heartaches and pain, but I made it!!

…and then follow it up with…Every time I turn around, God is blessing me….

~Keisha P.
Former Member of Word Harvest
Worship Center Church
Pomona, CA

I remember Carolyn:

When I think of the late Carolyn Harrell, I see her as a 21st century Esther. Carolyn was a real friend and a gracious, powerful woman of God. She impacted my life in so many ways that there aren't enough words to describe her.

One memorable happening in my life is when I was in a very critical hurting [time.] Not knowing what to do, Carolyn said, "Get off the phone, go to the airport and pick up your ticket. I will have someone meet you there and bring you to my house." Mind you now, she had houseguests there and there was a meeting going on at her church. She found the time, in the midst of what she had going on, to minister to me. She kept me at her home until she felt I was well enough to go back and face my situation. She waited on me herself.

She was a powerful speaker and anointed. She was witty and always had funny remarks to cheer you up at the right time. When the body of Christ lost Carolyn, we lost a great warrior that knew how to persevere.

Even now, when I am in a situation, what she shared with me still comes to mind and I am able to go on. Her prophetic words were on target. She never let anything stop her. She loved God and people. It is too bad the body of Christ did not realize it until it was too late.

Sure, we all have the strength of the Lord, but to hear [encouraging] words mean a lot. When we do not agree, let people know, "I might not agree, but I will stay with you until I know you are ok."

I wish we could have told her all the things we felt when she was alive. How she impacted our lives.

~Dr. Irene Huston
Pinole Community Worship Center
www.pinolecommunityworshipcenter.org
725 San Pablo Ave.
Pinole, CA 94564
(510) 724-4848

I remember Carolyn:

CAROLYN HARRELL, just the sound of her name brings a smile to my face. She was not like any other. Indeed she was a free spirit. There are not many days that pass without my thinking of her—her dedication to God; her smile; her wit; her generosity to all whom she loved; her love for her children and her grandchildren; and her all encompassing personality. She was funny, serious, disorganized as could be, but always able to poke fun at herself and others. She praised the Lord like none other; she was a preacher, a teacher, a lover of God's Word, and a blessing to countless thousands of people around the world. I cannot but remember, with joy in my heart, my friend forever, Dr. Carolyn Harrell. The times we spent together are numerous.... from pulpits, to parlors, to kitchens, to houses, Carolyn was my friend and she will always have a place in my heart where I will forever cherish our very special relationship. We were so very different, yet we loved and respected each other for our individual uniqueness. Until we meet again in heaven, I remain,

Your friend,

~Diana P. Cherry
From the Heart Church Ministries
Dr. John Cherry
Episcopal Pastor
44949 Allentown Road
Suitland, MD
www.fthm.org

Dr. Peggy R. Scott

Vignettes:
Scenes from the Cutting Room Floor

Vignette One

While Carolyn was busy raising her family, I completed my education, receiving a Bachelor of Arts degree in Political Science from Norfolk State University and Master's degree in Social Work (MSW) from Temple University. I also received a Master's of Arts in Biblical Studies from Jameson Christian College and a Doctorate of Divinity degree from International Christian University for life experience, education and ministry.

Vignette Two

When I was living in Washington, D.C. I was the victim of a robbery and attempted abduction of suspected rapists. I was on my way home from work when I saw a car about 500 yards ahead of me that had stopped. I could hear the music blasting. A voice spoke on the inside of me urging me to go on the porch of the house I was passing, suggesting that is where I lived. I rejected the voice (which I now know was the Holy Spirit) and continued walking towards the car. As I approached the car, they drove the car onto the sidewalk, blocking my path. As I attempted to walk around the car, the front passenger jumped out of the car and shoved a black nosed gun into my forehead demanding that I get into the car. It was a royal blue "Road Runner." As he shouted for me to get into the car, I had what I believe was a vision, a strong impression of me in the back seat and that I was going to be raped and killed. My immediate reaction was under no circumstances to get into the car. I would not exit alive. Even as the gunner held the gun on me I was saying, "Please, don't make me do this." He replied as I kept backing away from him, "what is wrong with you? Don't you see this?"

As he twisted the gun in my forehead, I begged, " Please don't..." All of a sudden the driver of the car leaned over and said, "Take her purse." I pushed it to the robber and he jumped into the car and drove away.

The reason I am sharing this story is because this experience profoundly impacted me to recommit my life to Christ, a few years later. I had accepted Jesus Christ as my Lord and Savior at the age of eight.

Vignette Three

Our mother and her siblings were raised by their grandmother in rural North Carolina. Grandma Martha, as she was called, was a woman of faith. I never met my grandmother or great grandmother but I heard the stories about her life of faith and dependency on God. Our mother told countless stories of how Grandma Martha was a worshipper and also a founding member of a church in Williamston, N.C. Those stories of faith became a family legacy. I believe she prayed for her grandchildren and their seeds' seed's which accounts for the numerous ministry gifts that God has raised up in our family. We are the answer to her prayers. Carolyn often preached about Grandma Martha's faith. I remember distinctly hearing the story about one winter when the temperature was low and the coal for the furnace had run out. According to family history, Grandma Martha went into her bedroom and knelt beside the bed. She always brought God an offering. She had one penny and she presented it to him and began to pray for the Lord to provide for "these children cause it is cold in this house." While she was praying a dump truck pulled up to the yard and emptied a truck load of coal that lasted them for many days. There were other stories of how they would find bags of groceries on their door step just in time to feed several hungry children.

Vignette Four

Our mother and stepfather had sold their home in New York and moved to California. She was a woman of prayer and reminded Carolyn that God revealed to her years ago that He was going to use her to reach many people with the gospel. That was when I really came to know my mother and found her to be a soft spoken (unlike Carolyn and myself), and a kind Christian woman. I believe today that it was all set up by Carolyn to get us together by the leading of the Holy Spirit. It was years before we talked about the disintegration of our family, and how the poverty impacted some of her decisions. Carolyn was forgiving and accepting of our mother all along. I still struggled with the abandonment, but Carolyn's love would always reach out to both of us. She was a repairer of the breach.

Biography of Dr. Peggy R. Scott

Dr. Peggy R. Scott is the founding Senior Pastor of *Fellowship Around the Word Church* located in Franklin, Virginia and the president of Peggy Scott Ministries, an apostolic and prophetic network of churches and ministries co-laboring to advance the kingdom of God and to fulfill the Great Commission. Dr. Scott is well respected by colleagues in the ministry and is considered by many to be a pastor to pastors within the body of Christ, regardless of religious affiliation, gender, or ethnicity. She is committed to encouraging, strengthening, and comforting leadership as directed by the Holy Spirit.

Having co-labored in the gospel for many years in California and extensively across the country and abroad with her sister, the late Dr. Carolyn Harrell, who was affectionately referred to as God's cheerleader to the body of Christ, Dr. Scott has "unforgettable" ministry experiences. On one occasion, she told a group of Los Angeles' gang members that Jesus is the "real homie." In tears, they rushed to the altar with their weapons and colors, surrendering and giving their hearts to Christ.

Dr. Scott is a contributing author to the book, *Those Preachin' Women, Volume I*, published by Dr. Ella P. Mitchell. Until recently she hosted a weekly television program, *Practical Truths: Real People, Real Issues* on WSKY4-TV and a motivational spot on 95.7 R&B station in the Hampton Roads Virginia (Norfolk, Virginia

Beach, Hampton, Newport News, Suffolk and surrounding areas). Recently, Dr. Scott rendered the invocation at the Virginia House of Delegates for the Commonwealth of Virginia.

Dr. Scott holds a Bachelor of Arts degree from Norfolk State University, a Master's Degree in Social Work (MSW) from Temple University, a Master of Arts in Biblical Studies from Jameson Christian College, and a Doctorate of Divinity degree from International Christian University for life experience, education, and ministry.